First World War
and Army of Occupation
War Diary
France, Belgium and Germany

8 DIVISION
24 Infantry Brigade,
Brigade Trench Mortar Battery
5 June 1915 - 16 March 1916

WO95/1723/3

The Naval & Military Press Ltd
www.nmarchive.com
Published in association with The National Archives

Published by

The Naval & Military Press Ltd

Unit 10 Ridgewood Industrial Park,

Uckfield, East Sussex,

TN22 5QE England

Tel: +44 (0) 1825 749494

www.naval-military-press.com

www.nmarchive.com

This diary has been reprinted in facsimile from the original. Any imperfections are inevitably reproduced and the quality may fall short of modern type and cartographic standards.

© **Crown Copyright**
Images reproduced by permission of The National Archives, London, England, 2015.

Contents

Document type	Place/Title	Date From	Date To
Heading	23 Div 24 Bde 24 Trench Mortar Bty 1915 June to 1916 Mar		
War Diary		05/06/1915	05/06/1915
War Diary	Ypres	06/06/1915	06/06/1915
War Diary	Hooge	07/06/1915	09/06/1915
Heading	G.H.G Troops 24th Trench How Batty RA Vol I 11-30.6.15		
War Diary	Ypres	11/06/1915	17/06/1915
War Diary	Poperinghe	18/06/1915	19/06/1915
War Diary	Hooge	20/06/1915	23/06/1915
War Diary	Poperinghe	24/06/1915	26/06/1915
War Diary	Hooge	27/06/1915	30/06/1915
War Diary	Ypres	01/07/1915	02/07/1915
War Diary	Poperinghe	03/07/1915	12/07/1915
War Diary	Hooge	13/07/1915	23/07/1915
War Diary	St Eloi	24/07/1915	24/07/1915
War Diary	Poperinghe	26/07/1915	29/07/1915
War Diary	St Eloi	30/07/1915	03/08/1915
War Diary	Wieltje	04/08/1915	15/08/1915
War Diary	Hooge	29/08/1915	30/11/1915
War Diary	In Action At St Eloi Portion Of 3rd Div Front In O2+O3 Map References Sheet 28	01/12/1915	31/12/1915
Heading	24 Trench Mortar Bty Jan Vol VII 3 Div		
War Diary	In Action At St Eloi Portion Of 3rd Div Front In O2+O3 Sheet 28	01/01/1916	23/01/1916
War Diary	St Eloi	25/01/1916	30/01/1916
Miscellaneous	D.A.G. Base	31/03/1916	31/03/1916
Miscellaneous	Reference War Diaries From My T.M. Batteries	22/03/1916	22/03/1916
Miscellaneous	Officer Commanding 24th Trench Mortar Battery	20/03/1916	20/03/1916
Heading	War Diary 24th T.M. Bty 1st Feb 1916 To 16th March 1916 Vol VIII		
War Diary	In Action At St Eloi Portion of 3rd Div Front O2+O3 Map Ref Sheet 28	01/02/1916	16/03/1916
Miscellaneous	Hd. Qts. 3rd Div	31/03/1916	31/03/1916
Miscellaneous	T.M.C Brigade Major 3rd D.A	06/04/1916	06/04/1916
Miscellaneous	Hd. Qts. 3rd Div	31/03/1916	31/03/1916

~~2 ARMY TROOPS~~

23 DIV

24 BDE

24 TRENCH MORTAR BY.

1915 JUNE TO 1916 MAR.

(1936)

WAR DIARY

INTELLIGENCE SUMMARY APPENDIX 11

Place	Date	Hour	Summary of Events and Information	Remarks and references to Appendices
	5.6.15		Left BERTHEN & proceeded to 3rd Divl. Hqs. as VLAMERTINGHE. Billetted with 40th BDE R.F.A. & M. Col. at BUSSEBOOM.	
YPRES	6.6.15		Went to 7th INF BDE Hqs and went down to the trenches after dark. Stayed in the trenches all next day & reconnoitred positions. Attached to WILTSHIRE REGT. Two guns & 12 men came up in the evening. No firing.	
HOOGE	7.6.15		Put guns into action.	
"	8.6.15		Germ. minenwerfer seems to have moved to flank. No firing	
"	9.6.15		One infantry working on repairs of emplacement. No firing fm. Working on alt.	

8

12/5935.

C. H. G. Shoote

24th Howler How" Battery R.A.

Vol I. 11 — 30.6.15.

Army Form C. 2118

WAR DIARY
or
INTELLIGENCE SUMMARY
(Erase heading not required.)

Place	Date	Hour	Summary of Events and Information	Remarks and references to Appendices
YPRES	11.6.15		Returned to 23rd BDE HM Col from HOOGE. Reconnoitred positions in front of 'Y' WOOD & RAILWAY WOOD.	
"	12.6.15 / 13.6.15		Nothing of importance	
"	14.6.15	10.30 pm	Took 4 guns into action in positions reconnoitred with 60 rds of Ammn. Carrying party from Bde A.T.'s took several rds.	
"	15.6.15		Laid out telephone wires & checked line etc of guns.	
"	16.6.15	3.20 am	Fired during Artillery bombardment till 4.15 am. Fired 36 rounds from 3 guns at wire in front of 'Y' WOOD. One gun out of action early in bombardment owing to lies breaking. 5g.7 DUCKS firing on trench EAST of RAILWAY WOOD went out of action after the 6th round with a bent chudding spindle. Howitzers fired all day after infantry attack. Gas shells used about 8 pm. the 3 guns hit in the dug out by one shrapnel.	
"	17.6.15		Stayed in action with one gun in case of counter attack. Took gun out of action in the evening & withdrew to Scots.	
POPERINGHE	18.6.15 / 19.6.15		Removal of battery resting in billets with 23rd ADEF R.A. Amn Col.	
HOOGE	20.6.15		Dug positions for two guns at HOOGE	
"	21.6.15		Took 2 guns into action at HOOGE with 20 rds.	

Army Form C. 2118

WAR DIARY
or
INTELLIGENCE SUMMARY
(Erase heading not required.)

Instructions regarding War Diaries and Intelligence Summaries are contained in F. S. Regs., Part II. and the Staff Manual respectively. Title Pages will be prepared in manuscript.

Place	Date	Hour	Summary of Events and Information	Remarks and references to Appendices
HOOGE	22.6.15	7.30pm	Fired 20 rounds at redoubt 200 yds WEST of CHATEAU during Artillery bombardment. At 8pm Infantry made an unsuccessful attack being held up by machine guns & bombs. When they had crossed the MENIN ROAD. Took guns out of action back to the ECOLE & personnel to 23rd BDE. am coll	
POPERINGHE	24/6/15 25.6.		to E.Mts. hen PAPPINGHE	
	26/6/15 27.6.15		Reconnoitred position for two Hows guns at HOOGE.	
HOOGE	28.6.15 1am		Dug position with Infantry fatigue party & brought 2 guns into action with 30 rounds to reply to German MINENWERFER. Fired two rounds in reply to MINENWERFER (completed) emplacements for other two guns. Brought up 40 rounds during night 28th–29th.	
	29.6.15 30.6.15		In action, waiting for German minenwerfer to open fire.	

1875 Wt. W593/826 1,000,000 4/15 J.B.C. & A. A.D.S.S./Forms/C. 2118.

Army Form C. 2118

WAR DIARY
or
INTELLIGENCE SUMMARY

24 Thench H. By
3rd Div.

(Erase heading not required.)

Place	Date	Hour	Summary of Events and Information	Remarks and references to Appendices
YPRES	1.7.15		Fired three rounds in reply to German Minenwerfer. Last round opened very effective & silenced the minenwerfer. Took guns out of action & hauled over 65 rounds to 14th Division. Left guns at ECOLE & withdrew personnel to 23rd Bde Am Col.	
POPERINGHE	2.7.15 3.7.15 4.7.15 5.7.15 6.7.15 7.7.15 8.7.15 9.7.15 10.7.15		In rest with 23rd Bde Am Col.	

S.G. Blundell 2/Lt RFA
O.C. 24th T.M. Bty

Army Form C. 2118

WAR DIARY
or
INTELLIGENCE SUMMARY
(Erase heading not required.)

2/4 Fd. Trench Hy. By.

Place	Date	Hour	Summary of Events and Information	Remarks and references to Appendices
POPERINGHE	11.7.15 12.7.15		In rest with 23rd BDE AMM COL.	
HOOGE	13.7.15 14.7.15 15.7.15 16.7.15 17.7.15		Went into action in old position at Hooge relieving 20th F.H. By. Fired a few registering rounds at the wall along MENIN Road. Fired single rounds at intervals during day & night both at the wall and the ANNEXE of rally to German mineshaft.	

S.G.Bleasch
2/LT R.F.A.
O.C. 2/4 F.T.H. By.

WAR DIARY
or
INTELLIGENCE SUMMARY

(Erase heading not required.)

Army Form C. 2118

24 July 1915

Place	Date	Hour	Summary of Events and Information	Remarks and references to Appendices
HOOGE	18.7.15		Fired a few rounds at intervals in reply to MINENWERFER.	
"	19.7.15	7 pm	We exploded a mine under German redoubt + immediately occupied the crater. While the infantry were consolidating their line, I fired in reply to MINENWERFER but was impeded by the spotting of an aeroplane and had to move positions. During the night and early morning of the 8th I fired both on the right + left sides of the crater lines hard to stopping the throwing of hand grenades shook. Very quiet. MINENWERFERS opened fire in the evening and did some damage. Fired a couple of rounds in reply on their trenches but could not take them on effectively owing to ammunition.	
"	20.7.15			
"	21.7.15		Got another 15 rounds. Three minenwerfers with different calibres on our front fired ammunition fire from three sides doing considerable damage. Fired in reply on their trenches but it only stops them temporarily. Fired a few rounds in reply to min.n wafer.	
	22.7.15 23.7.15		Relieved by 14th B.V.R. A.D.S.S./horns/C.2118 into rest near POPERINGHE. 3rd Div.	

Army Form C. 2118

WAR DIARY
or
INTELLIGENCE SUMMARY
(Erase heading not required.)

Place	Date	Hour	Summary of Events and Information	Remarks and references to Appendices
ST ELOI	24.7.16		Reconnoitred alternative positions in centre front of 3rd an 3rd Div line near ST ELOI.	

G.D.Marsh, Lt. R.F.A.
O.C. 24th T.M. Bty.

Army Form C. 2118

VIII ?   24.7.7. H/87

WAR DIARY
or
INTELLIGENCE SUMMARY
(Erase heading not required.)

Place	Date	Hour	Summary of Events and Information	Remarks and references to Appendices
POPERINGHE	26/7/15 to 29/7/15		In rest with 23rd BDE. A.M. Col. Recommended positions near ST ELOI. Hand over 2 guns to 20th T.H. 73½, & took over 2.1½" in return.	
ST ELOI	30/7/15		Came into action with them guns.	
	31/7/15		Nil.	
	1.8.15	3 am	Fired 3 2d at 3 1½" heavy at mound & mine craters at ST ELOI.	

1/8/15

E.A. Stuart [?] R.F.A.
O.C. 24th T.H. 73½

Army Form C. 2118

WAR DIARY
or
INTELLIGENCE SUMMARY
(Erase heading not required.)

24 H.7 H.8y

Place	Date	Hour	Summary of Events and Information	Remarks and references to Appendices
ST ELOI	2.8.15		Reconnoitred position N. of WIELTJE. German minenwerfer fired at 7pm Fired 4 rds in reply.	
"	3.8.15	10pm	moved 2 2" howitzers from ST ELOI to billets on the YSER CANAL	
WIELTJE	4.8.15	9.30pm	Took guns into action on 7th BDE Front. Fired two rounds at German trench opposite WIELTJE village.	
"	5.8.15		⎫	
"	6.8.15		⎬ Nil.	
"	7.8.15		⎪	
"	8.8.15		⎭	

K 20/4/15

G.W.Bhard
2/R.F.A
O.C. 24th T.H. OBy

Army Form C. 2118

WAR DIARY
or
INTELLIGENCE SUMMARY
(Erase heading not required.)

Instructions regarding War Diaries and Intelligence Summaries are contained in F.S. Regs., Part II. and the Staff Manual respectively. Title Pages will be prepared in manuscript.

24 T.I.A.B.

Place	Date	Hour	Summary of Events and Information	Remarks and references to Appendices
WIELTJE	9-8-15	2 am	Fired four rounds at German Sap.	
	10-8-15		Nil	
	11-8-15	3 am	Fired five rounds at German sap at request of infantry to reply to rifle grenades.	
	12-8-15		Nil	
	13-8-15	7.30 pm	Fired eight rounds. Ammunition expended. Withdrew detachment to Canal Bank.	
	14-8-15		Nil	
	15-8-15		Received 15 rounds from Am. Col. Went into action again.	

S.W. Shenley Maj.
O.C. 24 T.M.B.

Army Form C. 2118

WAR DIARY
or
INTELLIGENCE SUMMARY
(Erase heading not required.)

2/4 Trench Mortar Bty

Place	Date	Hour	Summary of Events and Information	Remarks and references to Appendices
Hooge	29.8.15 30.8.15 31.8.15 1.9.15 2.9.15		Mortars in position One in Bond street. One in B.8.	
	3.9.15	7.30pm	Withdrew gun from Bond St owing to shelling. Infantry had already withdrawn their men. Took gun and detachment back to dugouts by the 'Dump'.	
	4.9.15	9am	Fired one round from gun in Bond St in order to register. Same 6pm. Date 1/9/15. Moved gun from B8 to B3 by orders of the Brigadier, 9th Brigade. German mortar in wilno to the front of Grey House on the left of Stirling Castle. This mortar had done much damage. Orders only to fire in retaliation. Moved gun back to original position in Bond St.	

W. J. Morgan, 2 Lt R.G.A. for
O.C. 24th Trench Howitzer Battery.

Army Form C. 2118

24 T Fiwd How. Bg.

WAR DIARY
or
INTELLIGENCE SUMMARY
(Erase heading not required.)

Place	Date	Hour	Summary of Events and Information	Remarks and references to Appendices
HOOGE	4.9.15		Moved from to retaliate to MINENWERFER in SANCTUARY WOOD	
	5.9.15		Nothing to report.	
	6.9.15			
	7.9.15		Brought one gun into action to take on trenches between	
	8.9.15		HOOGE CHATEAU & BELLEWAARDE LAKE.	
	9.9.15			
	10.9.15		Nothing to report	
	11.9.15			

20/9/15

S. P. Bhand Maj. R.F.A.
O.C. 24th 1. H. Bg.

Army Form C. 2118

WAR DIARY
or
INTELLIGENCE SUMMARY
(Erase heading not required.)

24 T/medMTar T.

Place	Date	Hour	Summary of Events and Information	Remarks and references to Appendices
HOOGE	19		} Nothing to report.	
	20			
	21			
	22			
	23			
	24			
	25		Brought up guns and ammunition for attack.	
		3.50am	Commenced bombardment with ordinary bombs. Saved ammunition for future use in case of counter attacks etc. Fired a few smoke bombs to form smoke screen but as infantry were shrapnelled out of copings finches smoke screen was useless. One gun damaged by shell fire. Several rounds fired. Three casualties.	
	26		Very quiet day. Fired one round in the evening to silence German Trench Mortar.	

O.C. 24th T.M. Bty.

26/10/15

WAR DIARY or INTELLIGENCE SUMMARY

24th Trench Mortar Battery

Army Form C. 2118

Place	Date	Hour	Summary of Events and Information	Remarks and references to Appendices
24TH TRENCH BATTERY ATTACHED 3rd DIV	7.11.15		On this date the Bty was in action in ARMAGH WOOD (Sheet 28 I 30) being temporarily attd. 9th Div. Rest Billets at (G 22 Central) near BUSSEBOOM.	
	8th		The command of the Bty was taken over by MM CUDMORE 2Lieut R.F.A. vice Lieut MARSH R.F.A. who returned to his F.A. Brigade.	
	9th		By Corps order the personnel of the Bty. was withdrawn from action & all guns, gun-stores, ammunition etc handed over to 147th TRENCH BTY/	
	10th – 23rd		The personnel of the Bty. proceeded by motor-bus to STEENVOORDE rejoining 3rd Div at rest, & being attached 23rd B.A.C. for transport, returning etc. A rest programme of Physical Exercises, Route Marches, Visual Signalling etc was carried out.	18th Nov 32029 Gnr Roag R. RGA was admitted to hospital sick of the establishment.
	13th		2Lieut J.C. Dunn, one N.C.O. & two men proceeded to ABEELE to attend a Grenade Course. They rejoined on 21st.	
	22nd		O.C. proceeded with O.C. T.M. Btys 3rd Div to ST ELOI to reconnoitre new front.	

WAR DIARY or INTELLIGENCE SUMMARY

Army Form C. 2118

Place 24th TRENCH BTY
Summary of Events and Information ATTD 3rd DIV.

Date	Hour	Summary of Events and Information	Remarks
NOVEMBER 1915 24th		Half the Bty proceeded by motor-bus from STEENVOORDE to DICKEBUSCH thence on foot to St Eloi, relieved the 44th Trench Bty & came into action on the front held by 9th Inf. Bde in O2 & O3 Sheet 28. The guns etc of 44th Trench Bty were taken over & one emplacement was built but in an exposed position.	
25th		The relief half of Bty joined 40th B.A.C. & marched with them from STEENVOORDE to new billet near RENINGHELST (G 35 - d 9.1) The Bty is now attd. 40th R.B.A.C. for transport, rations etc.	
26th - 30th		A system of seven day reliefs is established. Work at once commenced on making emplacement & carried on vigorously. Owing however to the very serious state of the trenches progress is slow as most of the work can only be carried on at night. The Infantry moreover being extraordinarily busy on renovation work themselves find great difficulty in lending assistance, & have urgently requested that no shooting be done at present.	

Jno Gregson Lt RFA
O.C. 24th Trench Bty

WAR DIARY or INTELLIGENCE SUMMARY

Army Form C.2118

24th Trench Mortar Battery

Place: 24th TRENCH BTY ATTD 3rd DIV

Date December	Hour	Summary of Events and Information	Remarks and references to Appendices
1st 16th		Work is carried on continuously building emplacements. This work has chiefly to be done at night, owing to the exposed nature of the position & the exceptionally bad state of the communication trenches & as therefore necessarily slow. A small hut is also erected at rest billets for the use of the rear half of the battery.	No. 6396 Pte Armstrong 1st N.F. Evacuated sick 3.12.15
	11th	The infantry thing at length agitated 8 rounds were fired at dusk on enemy front line & cottages E. of Mound. Two kinds of Lewis fired with 3rd fired from S.Bags were both Churd. AM Thus detonated (with).	No. 12210 Pte Tasker A + No. 9457 Pte Hammond H. 4 R.R.F. joined 6.12.15
	14th	On the night 13th–14th one man was unluckily hit by a stray bullet while filling Sandbags. Orland support trenches.	No. 16609 Pte Baker F.W. 1st Nor. joined 10.12.15
	15th	Three rounds fired to register from new 2" emplacement at	5029 Pte McCabe wounded 1st Nor. 12.15
	17th	0.2 a.m.	
		Telephonic communication established between night positions of guns & central dug-out. Ammunition brought up etc.	13208 Pte Houghton 16 R.W.F. joined 15.12.15

Map References:
3rd Div Trench Map O.1.O.3
Sheet 28

In action at St Eloi, Ration of

WAR DIARY or INTELLIGENCE SUMMARY

Army Form C. 2118

Place	Date	Hour	Summary of Events and Information	Remarks and references to Appendices
24th TRENCH BATTERY ATTD 3rd DIV	1915 DECEMBER 18th		By arrangement with G.O.C. INF. BDE two guns were brought to bear on a forward enemy trench at O.2.d.6.8. & 23 rounds fired. The 2" Platform sank in the mud but the 15" shot with considerable accuracy. At 5.30 A.M. the battery stood to owing to enemy gas attack further north but all remained quiet on our sector. A small amount of lachrymatory gas was noticed.	10407 Pte O'Hare 2nd R.I.R. found 18.12.15
	19th		During afternoon the Fd. guns attempted to cut wire in front of forward enemy trench referred to above. 10 r dropped over 1½" bombs intermittently during night 20th-21st to harass any attempts at repairing. The enemy responded with rifle grenades but these were silenced.	
	20th		The enemy's retaliation seems generally to be very slight.	

R. Cadmore Lt R.F.A.
O.C. 24th Trench T.Bty.

3rd Div Ford in O.2.b.9.
Map Reference Sht 28

Army Form C. 2118

WAR DIARY
or
INTELLIGENCE SUMMARY
(Erase heading not required.)

Instructions regarding War Diaries and Intelligence Summaries are contained in F. S. Regs., Part II. and the Staff Manual respectively. Title Pages will be prepared in manuscript.

Place	Date	Hour	Summary of Events and Information	Remarks and references to Appendices
24th TRENCH BATTERY ATTD 3rd DIV	1915 DECEMBER 23.		2" Gun was registered on 2 new forward Trenches on mound. Registration being necessary owing to tied heaving the mound since last time the gun was fired.	
	24.		9 Rounds 15" were fired during afternoon from position behind R 3, & 4 rounds 2" from "Shelly Farm" position, on to the new forward Trenches on Mound & on to the trench portion of Mound. One trench 2" received a direct hit damage, good damage of new timber, previously in situ. Enemy retaliated with about six small trench mortar bombs or Rifle Grenades two of which were blinds, no damage was done. Our Infantry retaliated with Rifle Grenades.	See note following 3/2/
	25.		Instructions received yesterday for a Bombardment today, to once cancelled. Inspection was very quiet during the whole day. Enemy hairyweered the front trench lines in "Victoria Court" during last night, we had no gun fire tonight. Instructions received from BDE. H.Q. that bombardment arranged for today would be carried out tomorrow.	
	26.		Fired 7 Rounds 2" from B position – Shelly Farm, 3 Rounds 2" from "B" & Third R.2, & 3 Rounds from behind R.3. owing to the bad state of the ground at R.3 it was found advisable to discontinue firing from that position as the Gun bed was moving. After 300 Round from "B" the timber under bed was broken. Both beds and gun emplacements were rebuilt during the night. Enemy retaliation was very slight.	

3rd Div Ind x Q2 x Q3
Map References Sheet 28

Sn Letter of STELA Retn of

Army Form C. 2118

WAR DIARY
or
INTELLIGENCE SUMMARY
(Erase heading not required.)

Instructions regarding War Diaries and Intelligence Summaries are contained in F. S. Regs., Part II. and the Staff Manual respectively. Title Pages will be prepared in manuscript.

Place	Date	Hour	Summary of Events and Information	Remarks and references to Appendices
2nd Trench Howitzer Batty	1915 December		ATTD 3RD DIV.	
	27.	M.M.	2 H.E. bombard. 1 Schrap & 1 Smoke fired at 3o Div Barrack Schrap to distract snipers in Guereade works &c. "A" & "B" positions were shelled but no damage was done.	See Note on 5th Nov 1915.
	28.		The wind being in a favourable direct for the enemy gas precautions were duly taken. Front refacing there Head Quarters drys out during the Day; also making fires experimental Implement for Gun Post.	
	29.		During the Day seven but more small calibre shells passed "A" position a few near "B". Both positions seem to have been located. During the night 29 5/30 & men sleeping at "A" position report that Very Lights & occasional Rifle Grenade or minent. Sent over their position by the Enemy. No damage was done.	
	30		During the morning the neighbourhood & dugt. visited "A" position were immediately fired upon by the enemy with air "whizz Bangs". No damage was done. The position is evidently under observation by the enemy & thought not accessible to fire from that position for some time. The position is in view of the Enemy on our extreme Left. New observation Post for 2" Gun carried from T.M.C. 3o Div.	

1875 Wt. W593/826 1,000,000 4/15 J.B.C. & A. A.D.S.S./Forms/C. 2118.

WAR DIARY or INTELLIGENCE SUMMARY

Army Form C. 2118

Place: 2/Lt Tweedie Howitzer Bitty   ATTD 3RD DIV

Date: 1915 December

Date	Hour	Summary of Events and Information	Remarks
30		(contd) T.M.C. reported that our Daily Reports to 3rd D.A. had not been received for the past three days. This has been cont. despatch was traced to James Brigade (Infantry) H.Q. Sergt Masterman instructing two men now to the Battery, the one being 9.15 firs	
31		During the evening this Coy/ continued the tuition to men who requiring 1⁵ instrument.	
		2/Lt JCBrown retired to D.H. Castle Redoubt plainly of from. It was thought that one bomb exploded on a soft there it shifted many sand bags & shook the ground considerably, other damage was also done.	J.C.Brown at 3rd Donald Batt. to Journal 2/Lt

In action at St Eloi — In position of 3rd Div face at 02 y 03 and Reserve Sheet 28.

9.4 Inch Mortar Bty
Jan
Vol VII

3 Sri

24th Trench Mortar Battery

Army Form C. 2118

WAR DIARY or INTELLIGENCE SUMMARY

17/1/16 ATTD 3rd DIV

Place	Date 1916	Hour	Summary of Events and Information	Remarks and references to Appendices
24 R TRENCH BATTERY	January 1st		At midnight 31st–1st the enemy became very nervous, sending up very numerous star lights, opening rapid fire, the latter went answered by Bursts of rapid fire. Work was carried out during the day on A, Platform.	
	2		Work on A, + fired from E to register. In enemy front line trench first shot.	
	3		Work on B, preparing ground etc	
	4		Put in Platform at B,. Fired from A, to register on enemy front line. 5th. Preparation of concussive tamper taking place in rear. One shot Mortar Pups a range position at least 20 yds long.	
	5		Work preparing ground for E, Platform + making improvement at E, Tunnel. Fired at C on L of new firing line. Firing to register from A,, B, + C. At night the 2nd A, was replaced by 12.	
	6		Protection built for A, + the platforms at A, + B, strengthened. Work at relaying telephone wires by night.	
	7		Firing from A,, B,, + C to register. Work on E + E,	

In action at St Eloi, portion of 3rd Div front + 3rd Bde, Sect 8a

WAR DIARY
or
INTELLIGENCE SUMMARY
(Erase heading not required.)

Army Form C. 2118

Place	Date	Hour	Summary of Events and Information	Remarks and references to Appendices
24th TRENCH BATTERY ATTD 3rd DIV	JANUARY 7/16	8th	Work commenced on E1 & A1 but R1 was rendered by enemy shell-fire which destroyed dugouts of R1 already constructed by Trench Mortar Bty. Fired to register.	8.1.16 Transferred from 24th T.M.B. 7712 (A) Baker R.S.F. 8165 (a) Moss 2 RIR 4618 Pte Bingham " 4089 " Lang " 16620 Pte Brown 4 R.R. 14609 " Baker 1 NF Joined 9.1.16 Lieut (A) Wilson R.W.F. 14106 Bn McMahon " 3149 G/Cpl R.O.P. West " Turner " 14608 " Woodend " 5159 " Moore " from 43rd T.M.B. 9.1.16 7524 G/Cpl Firkin R.D.F. 5769 " Thomas " 5767 " Light " from BERTHEN 11.1.16 29951 Cpl Maloney " S761 Gn Caffrey " 59172 " Cabin "
		9th	Preparations for combined offensive operation with 9th Inf Bde. 2" gun brought up to E1 M	
		10th	"Stood to" at 2 AM for covering of grenade attack. This was delayed by the parties not digging their correct positions within radius, until ten minutes to four by which time the enemy were aware that an attack was made to our party of were made to give no definite information as to the return of the party into our line centre. Guns did not come into play as the enemy did much damage to our support line and seated us advantageously for our bombarded our support line. B1 was severely located as it mortars along all places etc. Treatment, however 2nd came in for special treatment. Fired 15 rounds in retaliation. Gun removed.	
		11th	Built new dugout for men in R1 trench as Priem had been knocked in by Trench Mortar. Repairing B1.	

A.R. Cadmore Capt R.F.A.
O.C. 24th T.M.B.

WAR DIARY
or
INTELLIGENCE SUMMARY
(Erase heading not required.)

Army Form C. 2118

Place	Date	Hour	Summary of Events and Information	Remarks and references to Appendices
January 1916	24th	12th	TRENCH BATTERY ATTD 3rd DIV	

T.M. Batteries having been re classified as Medium, Light etc transfers of personnel have taken place. This battery was this day completed to full strength in gunners. The transfers have been as follows:-

Posted to 43rd (Light) T.M.B. 8.1.16.

8165 Cpl Moran G 2nd R.I.R 6618 Pt Colquhoun A 2nd R.I.R.
7712 Cpl Baker A 1st R.S.F. 16609 Pte Baker A.E 1st N.F.
6989 Rfn Law T 2nd R.I.R.   16620 " Boroden 4th R.F.

Posted to 26th T.M.B from 43rd T.M.B. 8.1.16

56036 Cpl Wilkinson V R.F.A 57239 Gr Moore H R.G.A.
59134 Br M?Munn E "   44027 " Turner W "
34999 Gr Cooke J. R.G.A   46608 " Woodhead W.S "

Posted to 26th T.M.B. from BERTHEN 9.1.16 4526 Gr Fisher RGA 5160 Gr Lock 5406 Gr Hannen
19.1.16. 23931 Cpl Mahoney H RGA S-9172 Gr Cobain RGA 5982 Gr Shelley RGA
On this date also 75691 Bm Cecon on leave from 4.1.16 became
an absentee & 72223 Gr Batt RFA was evacuated sick

In billets at St Eloi posh'n of 3rd Div
Mob RFA Shed 28

WAR DIARY
or
INTELLIGENCE SUMMARY

Army Form C. 2118

Place	Date	Hour	Summary of Events and Information	Remarks and references to Appendices
January 1916			**24th TRENCH BTY ATTD 3rd DIV**	
	13th		Work on emplacements & repairs to dug-outs, bringing up sand-bags, timber, etc.	
	15th		Work on E in T.T.	
	16th		Put in 1½" Ted in new position (A2) in R1. Bringing up ammunition etc.	
	17th		Work on A2. Fired 6 rounds from A1 in retaliation & silenced enemy mortar.	
	18th		2 Lieut Dunn to England. Put in experimental 2" Ted on Trevor. Put in experimental 2" Ted at A1. Fired to register on enemy forward post from C.	20.1.16 53168 G. Whittaker RGA Posted from BERTHEN
	19th		Fired to register.	
	21st		Enemy retaliated on R trenches. Were responded with a few from A1. New bed satisfactory. This should stir up the enemy rate.	
	23rd		By arrangement with 9th T.B. Bty the covert wire turned on enemy forward trench opp. R3, & fired at 2.30 p.m. 16 rounds. The object was to doing a great deal of damage to wire & trench. The enemy	

Army Form C. 2118

WAR DIARY
or
INTELLIGENCE SUMMARY
(Erase heading not required.)

Instructions regarding War Diaries and Intelligence Summaries are contained in F.S. Regs., Part II. and the Staff Manual respectively. Title Pages will be prepared in manuscript.

Place	Date	Hour	Summary of Events and Information	Remarks and references to Appendices
St Eloi	Jan 25th		Spent afternoon relieving Trench Howitzers.	
"	Jan 26th		Moved 2" guns from Q.3 to R.3. Dugouts in R.1 were shelled. Two blown in, party of trench.	
"	27th		Captain Ayles, 2nd Lieut. Keene + 2 other ranks the victims. Showed them moved. Started dugouts in Convent Lane.	
"	28th		Sergts shelled about 4:30 P.M.	
"	29th		Quiet day. Tried 6 inch trench bomb at M.G. emplacement, no retaliation.	
"	30th		Foggy day. Relieved by Lieut Dunn.	

D.A.G.
Base

I enclose War Diary of
24th Trench Mortar Battery from
1st Feby 1916 to 18th March 1916

This is sent you by direction
of Brigade Major, 3rd D.A.

AB Cab
CAPT.
T.M.C.
3RD DIVN.

22/3/16 O.C. 24" Mortar Bttys

War Diaries are made by
months & not to run into the next.
Attention is called to C.R. 140/592
dated 17.12.16 & Para 140 Field
Service Regulations Part II. If a Battery
is on the line for say 14 days & out 14 days A.F.
2118 should read 1-14 March in billets 15-30
giving daily occurrences
G.H.Q.
3rd Echelon   H Yates Capt D.A.A.G.
31. 3. 16

G 490

Adjt Captain
3rd D.A.

Reference war diaries from
my T.M. Batteries —

Shall these be sent to you
in futures & shall they be sent
direct to A.G. Base

A d Fox
CAPT,
T.M.O.
3RD DIVN.

21/3/16.

T.M.C.

Direct to the D.A.G., Base,
please.

D M Graham
Capt R.A.
B.M. 3rd D.A.

22/3/16.

Officer Commanding
2nd Trench Mortar Battery

I herewith return attached War Diary. We cease to be responsible for the administration of Batteries from todays date 20-3-16

20 3/16

Lieut. R.F.A.
Adjt. Trench Mortar School
2nd Army

WAR DIARY
24th T.M.B'ty
1st FEB 1916
to
16th March 1916

Vol VIII

Army Form C. 2118

WAR DIARY
or
INTELLIGENCE SUMMARY
(Erase heading not required.)

Summary of Events and Information 3RD Div

Place	Date	Hour		Remarks and references to Appendices
February 1916	24TH		Trench Mortar Batty.	
			Work carried on in Reserve position in old Trench - Victoria Street. The position previously chosen for Reserve Dug-out was thought to be unsuitable. Another place was decided upon in R.6. Had two men collecting material to together for repairing trench leading from C.T. (Bonnet Lane) to dug site for Dug-out.	
	2nd		Arrangements made with officer in charge of King's L'pool Pioneer Party, to exchange sand Bags filled by us, for a small party of his men to fill sand Bags for us from our Dug-out site for men repairing Trench R.6. Arranged with Intelligence Officer R. Scots to fire a few rounds at enemy observation working post on east of Moevres. After firing pre-arranged number of rounds enemy retaliated with Trench Mortars, Rifle Grenades & we answered frig's. Finally he turned on his field Guns. which was probably intended to deceive a small party of Infantry walking along road leading to Trenches. 8 Rounds fired from A.1. position - e.g. New behrmenthal 2" Bat, which work satisfactory. 2 Rounds from C. 13"	

In action at 24th 8401 portion of
3RD Div. Front O. v O.
Map ref: Sheet 28

Army Form C. 2118

(15)

WAR DIARY
or
INTELLIGENCE SUMMARY
(Erase heading not required.)

Summary of Events and Information 24TH TRENCH MORTAR Bd ☒ 3RD DIV

Place	Date	Hour	Summary of Events and Information	Remarks and references to Appendices
February	3rd		been working on new Dug-out & Trench. Enemy Heavy Trench Mortars made their appearance on our front this morning, about 8 o'clock they fired three or four rounds which fell in field behind R.2.S. Infantry in Trenches did not wait for immediate retaliation. Work continued on Dug-out & Trench R.6.	
	4th		Work on new dug-out in R.6 & on F emplacement. Enemy Heavy minenwerfer opened fire at 7.10 A.M but ceased after we had fired a few back. Very considerable artillery activity all day.	
	5th		Enemy heavy minenwerfer again opened at 7.25 A.M., with two guns. We retaliated with 25-12# were assisted by the field guns. F position completed & Newton fired on Enemy in north Bend Trin. 2090 R & VOORMEZEELE Church Tower covering Enemy front line night of MOUND.	4. CHURCHILL to ENGLAND on leave

In Action at ST ELOI Position of 3rd D.W. Front Ca & Da Map Ref Sheet 28

Army Form C. 2118

WAR DIARY
or
INTELLIGENCE SUMMARY
(Erase heading not required.)

Instructions regarding War Diaries and Intelligence Summaries are contained in F.S. Regs., Part II. and the Staff Manual respectively. Title Pages will be prepared in manuscript.

Place	Date	Hour	Summary of Events and Information	Remarks and references to Appendices
February 1916	7th		24th TRENCH BTY ATTD 3rd DIV Enemy quiet. Found dud thrown by him yesterday morning — a rather long-nosed shell with brass fuze (broken off), about 2'3" long, diameter just over 6", estimated weight 120 lbs, no driving band, but 6 large flat studs, copper or brass, near base.	
	8th		The battery was relieved by some T.M personnel of 17th Div. who only arrived in time to allow our own men to reach Winnezeele at 12.30 A.M. 8th–9th.	
	9th		The battery having handed over all guns, gun-stores, ruts, pack-saddles etc, moved off with 23rd B.A.C. at 8. A.M and proceeded by road to Zermezeele.	
	10th		Moved with 23rd B.A.C. by road from Zermezeele to Guemy.	
	11th		Marched from Guemy to Winnezeele at Tournehem.	

Army Form C. 2118

WAR DIARY
or
INTELLIGENCE SUMMARY   February
(Erase heading not required.)

Place	Date 1916	Hour	Summary of Events and Information 2nd S. Brewers	Remarks and references to Appendices
February	26		2/6 French Battery	(1)
			All TM Regs of Divisional Brigaded under TMC at TOURNEHEM for training purposes.	
			No gun exercise but carried on with marching drill.	
			Physical exercise, Bomb throwing and inspection.	
	16		Lt. J.L. Evans transferred to C. of newly formed 59th T.M.B.	
			Lt. E.C. Douglas R.G.A. posted to Reneup in his place.	
	17		M.M. Enamore took over duties of T.M.C. during absence of Capt. Cole. Lt. E.C. Douglas acting F.C. Reneup	

WAR DIARY
or
INTELLIGENCE SUMMARY

Army Form C. 2118

March

Place	Date	Hour	Summary of Events and Information	Remarks and references to Appendices
Winnezeele Railway			H.Q. 2nd Division	
	9/3		First Echelon returned to duty with Railway vehicles marched with 42nd T.M.C. to PALEMBERG via WATTEN	
	10/3		O.C. Proceeded on to NIEPPEBUSCH to make arrangements for Battery going into action.	
	11/3		Battery marched with 42nd T.M.C. to Canvis Street near RENINGHELST.	

WAR DIARY
INTELLIGENCE SUMMARY

Army Form C. 2118

Month: March

Place	Date	Hour	Summary of Events and Information	Remarks and references to Appendices
24 R TRENCH BATTERY ATTD 3rd DIV	March 1916	7a	Half the battery proceeded to trenches and relieved 17 R.Div. T.M.B. Remainder in front we relieved previously.	
	12		G 35 d 9.1 and attd 23rd B.A.C for rations & transport as before. Moved 2" from unsatisfactory position at O 2.2 86 near Cellar Lane to SDT F bastion O 2 a 68.5½, drained off water from incomplete French dug-out to R.b. & commenced recovering ammunition. A large stock was buried over & no amount of which was nor need of water.	
	13			
	14		8th digging out bombs. Received 2" bombs from Corps filled with nitrokleksum. Sent down one without fuse. Constructed new bomb store at VOORMEZEELE as one in use was leaking & collapsing. S.B.I. recovering bombs.	
	15		Got up some new ammunition to replace damaged stock. Huns keeping very quiet & we are taking no offensive action.	
	16			

R.A. Crelmore Lt RFA
O.C. 24 R T.M.B

Sub-Section at ST ELOI. Position of 3rd Div Front = O 2 + O 2
Map Ref. Sheet 28

CONFIDENTIAL

T M

A.G.'s OFFICE AT THE BASE
CENTRAL REGISTRY
-2 APR 1916
C.R. No. 140/1077

Hd. Qts.,
  3rd Div:

1.

The attached War Diary is returned with the request that the Officer commanding may be instructed to compile A.F. C 2118 in accordance with instructions contained in para.140 Field Service Regulations, Part II.

The period 1st - 17th February and 9th - 16th March is only taken into account.

Attention is invited to C.R.140/592 dated 12/12/15 which clearly states War Diaries are to be submitted for complete months.

G.H.Q., 3rd Echelon.
31/3/1916.

Major-General,
D. A. G., 3rd Echelon.

2.

C.R.A.

Will you please instruct the O.C. 24. T.M. Battery to complete his February diary and also that for March and send them in again, in separate covers.

4.3.16. **P.T.O**

R. Dunlop Maj.
D.A.Q.M.G. 3 Div

3

TMC

Please comply early

D McGraham
Capt BM
5/4/16 3rd D.A.

4

Brigade Major
3rd D.A.

Both the officers of this Battery are casualties - one injured 23/3/16 one killed 27/3/16 - I regret there is no one in a position to complete the War Diary. I have separated the months.

6/4/16

A W Gab
CAPT.
T.M.O.
3RD DIVN.

D.A.G. Base

War Diary herewith. Owing to casualties the diary cannot be completed.

D McGraham
Capt Bde Major
3rd Div Art.

13/4/16

Hd. Qts.,
    3rd Div:

A.G.'s OFFICE AT THE BASE
CENTRAL REGISTRY
-2 APR 1916
C.R. No. 140/1077

    The attached War Diary is returned with the request that the Officer commanding may be instructed to compile A.F. C 2118 in accordance with instructions contained in para.140 Field Service Regulations, Part II.

    The period 1st - 17th February and 9th - 16th March is only taken into account.

    Attention is invited to C.R.140/592 dated 12/12/15 which clearly states War Diaries are to be submitted for complete months.

                          (SD.) EDW. GRAHAM.

G. H. Q., 3rd Echelon.   Major-General,
31/3/1916.   D. A. G., 3rd Echelon.

www.ingramcontent.com/pod-product-compliance
Lightning Source LLC
Chambersburg PA
CBHW081458160426
43193CB00013B/2530